THIRD EDITION

2

LET'S

WORKBOOK

GO

Elaine Cross

Ritsuko Nakata

Karen Frazier

Barbara Hoskins

OXFORD
UNIVERSITY PRESS

Let's Start

A. Read, trace, and write.

Hi, Kate. How are you?

Good-bye, Kate.

I'm OK, thanks.
How about you?

Pretty good!

See you later!

____, Andy. How are ____?

Good-bye, Andy.

Pretty good, thanks.
How about you?

OK.

____ you ____!

| you | Hi | OK | See | I'm | later |

B. Look, unscramble, and write.

1. rease het orabd

   erase the board

2. tiewr ym aenm

3. dera kosbo

4. ekspa slignEh

C. Look and write.

1.

GINGER

I write my name

at school.

2.

My name is Sam.

_I_

at school.

3.

4.

NGER

.

.

✓

Let's Learn

A. Trace and match.

1. a workbook
2. a paper clip
3. a calendar
4. a clock
5. a pencil sharpener
6. a window
7. a picture
8. a door

B. Read and circle.

1. This is a door.

2. That's a clock.

3. This is a workbook.

4. That's a pencil sharpener.

C. Trace and write.

1.

What's this?

It's a paper clip.

2.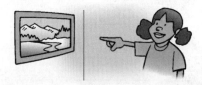

What's that?

.

3.

?

It's a door.

4.

?

It's a .

D. Read, trace, and write.

1. Is this a picture?

Yes, it is.

2. Is that a workbook?

No, it isn't.

3. Is this a clock?

.

4. Is that a window?

.

✓

Let's Learn More

A. Look and write.

1.

   Those are clocks.

2.

   These are .

3.

   .

4.

   .

5.

   .

6.

   .

B. Write.

1. This is a window. ➡ These are windows.

2. That is a calendar. ➡ Those are .

3. This is a door. ➡ .

4. That is a picture. ➡ .

C. Read and match.

1. What are these?
   They're pencil sharpeners.

2. What are those?
   They're doors.

3. What are those?
   They're pictures.

4. What are these?
   They're workbooks.

D. Connect, trace, and write.

1. Are these windows?

   No, they aren't.

2. Are these _____?

   Yes, they are.

3. _____ pencil sharpeners?

   _____.

4. _____ pictures?

   _____.

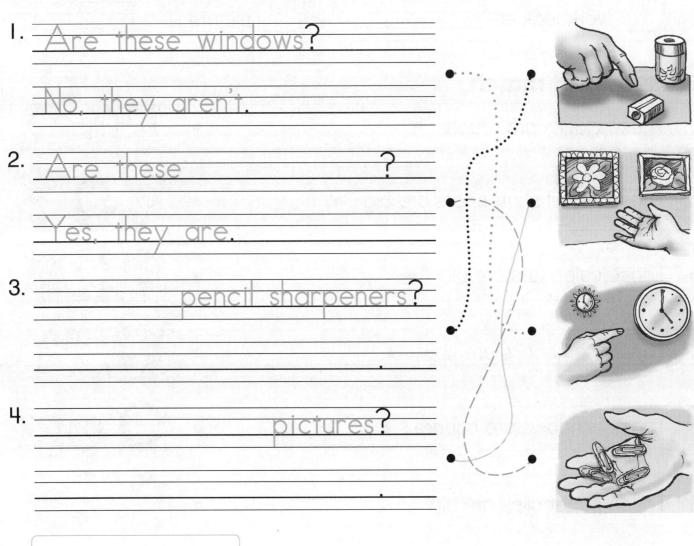

Let's Build

A. Circle and write.

1.

little

big

| This
That | door is | ~~little~~. |

2.

square

round

| This
That | window is | _____. |

3.

old

new

| This
That | workbook is | _____. |

4.

long

short

| This
That | picture is | _____. |

B. Read and match.

1. These clocks are round. •

2. These pencil sharpeners are big. •

3. Those calendars are old. •

4. These workbooks are new. •

5. Those windows are square. •

6. These paper clips are big. •

C. Look and check.

1.

☐ This bicycle is long.
☐ That bicycle is long.

2.

☐ These erasers are square.
☐ Those erasers are square.

D. Unscramble and write.

1. are clocks Those big

Those clocks are big.

2. small This rabbit is

3. pencils long are These

4. is square That door

5. new is picture This

6. Those round are calendars

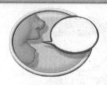

Let's Start

A. Read and write.

1.

Whose bag is that?

_____
_____ .

2.

_____ ?

_____
_____ .

| It's his bag. | It's her bag. | Whose bag is that? |

B. Look and write.

1.

_____ bag is _____ ?

It's _____ .

| bag |
| Whose |
| Scott's |
| that |

2.

Whose bag _____ ?

It's _____ .

| is |
| Jenny's |
| that |
| bag |

C. Read and match.

1. He can sing.   •

2. She can dance.   •

3. She can run.   •

4. He can swim.   •

D. Look and write.

1.

He can _____ .

2.

She _____ .

3.

She _____ .

4.

He _____ .

✓

Let's Learn

A. Look and write.

1.

   a tissue

2.

3.

4.

5.

6.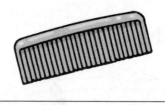

a comb
a watch
a tissue
a brush
a key
a coin

B. Draw and write.

What do you have?

I have a _____.

C. Trace and write.

(A)

1. I have a candy bar.

2. _____.

3. _____.

(B)

1. _____ a comic book.

2. _____.

3. _____.

D. Read and circle.

1. Do you have a key?

Yes, I do.

No, I don't.

2. Do you have a comb?

Yes, I do.

No, I don't.

3. Do you have a comic book?

Yes, I do.

No, I don't.

4. Do you have a watch?

Yes, I do.

No, I don't.

✓

Let's Learn More

A. Unscramble and write.

1. ulcalaortc

   calculator

2. tlalew

   _____

3. rembulal

   _____

4. uchln bxo

   _____

5. yek hican

   _____

6. ntria ssap

   _____

7. marace

   _____

8. simuc alyerp

   _____

> camera
> key chain
> music player
> calculator
> train pass
> umbrella
> lunch box
> wallet

B. Connect and write.

1.

2.

3.

4.

5.

She has a camera.

C. Trace and write.

1.

What does she have?

She has a lunch box.

2.

he have?

.

3.

?

.

D. Trace, write, and check.

 (1)    (2)    (3)    (4)

1. Does he have a lunch box?

☑ Yes, he does.
☐ No, he doesn't.

2. a comb?

☐ Yes, she does.
☐ No, she doesn't.

3. a music player?

☐ Yes, he does.
☐ No, he doesn't.

4. a calculator?

☐ Yes, she does.
☐ No, she doesn't.

Let's Build

A. Trace and write.

1. She has _____ in her bag.

2. _____ in his bag.

B. Trace and write.

1. What does she have in her hand?
   She has a comic book in her hand.

2. _____ he have in his hand?
   _____ comb in his hand.

3. _____?
   _____ brush _____.

4. _____?
   _____ music player _____.

C. Read and check.

1. Does he have a camera in his bag?

   ☐ Yes, he does.

   ☑ No, he doesn't.

2. Does he have a watch in his bag?

   ☐ Yes, he does.

   ☐ No, he doesn't.

3. Does she have a wallet in her bag?

   ☐ Yes, she does.

   ☐ No, she doesn't.

4. Does she have a CD in her bag?

   ☐ Yes, she does.

   ☐ No, she doesn't.

D. Draw and write.

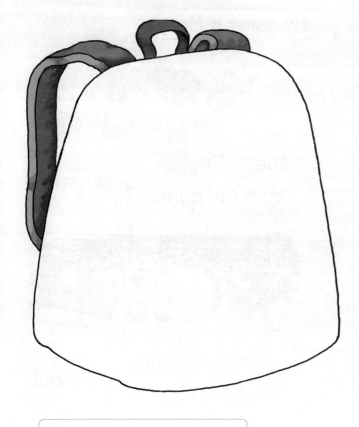

What do you have in your bag?

1. I have _____.

2. _____.

3. _____.

☐ ✓

Units 1-2 Listen and Review

A. Read and match.

1. What are these?

2. What does he have in his hand?

3. Does she have a watch?

4. Whose bag is that?

It's his bag.

Yes, she does.

They're windows.

He has a train pass in his hand.

B. Read and circle.

1.

He can ~~swim.~~ sing.

2. My name is Mary.

I speak English write my name at school.

3.

She can dance. run.

4.

I erase the board read books at school.

Let's Learn About Numbers 20-100

A. Match.

thirty	21
twenty-four	29
forty	70
twenty-two	20
twenty-five	50
seventy	26
twenty-one	100
ninety	24
twenty-nine	22
one hundred	40
sixty	25
twenty-three	80
twenty	27
twenty-six	30
twenty-eight	60
eighty	23
twenty-seven	28
fifty	90

B. Count and write.

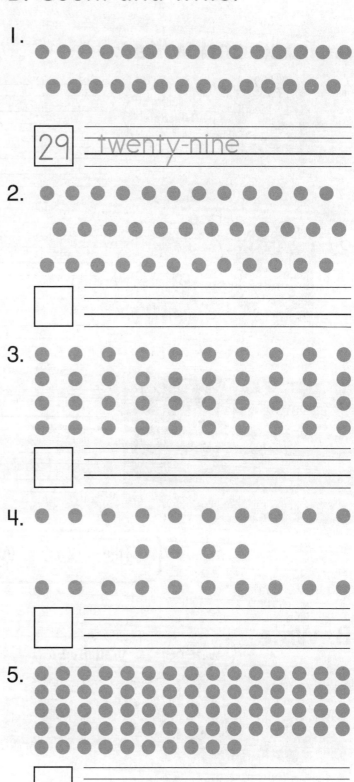

1.

‖29‖ twenty-nine

2.

3.

4.

5.

✓

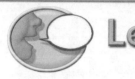

Let's Start

A. Trace and write.

1.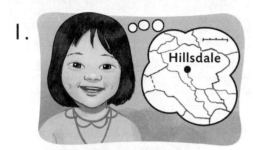

Where do you live?

I _____ in Hillsdale.

2.

What's _____ address?

_____ 16 North Street.

3.

(798) 555-2043

_____ your cell phone number?

It's (798) 555-2043.

It's   live   What's   your

B. Write.

Where do you live?

_____
_____
_____
_____.

C. Read and check.

1. What can he do?
   - [ ] He can use chopsticks.
   - [✓] He can do a magic trick.

2. What can she do?
   - [ ] She can ice-skate.
   - [ ] She can play baseball.

3. What can he do?
   - [ ] He can ice-skate.
   - [ ] He can do a magic trick.

4. What can she do?
   - [ ] She can use chopsticks.
   - [ ] She can play baseball.

D. Draw and write.

What can you do?

I can _____ .

I can _____ .

Let's Learn

A. Look and write.

6.
8.
2.
1. | s | t | o | v | e |
3.
7.
4.
5.

bed
bathtub
sofa
stove
sink
TV
refrigerator
toilet

Across

1.   2.   3.

4.   5.

Down

6.   7.

8.

B. Look, trace, and write.

1.   The lamp is in the bedroom.

2.    kitchen.

3.    living room.

C. Read and check.

1. Where's the telephone?
   It's in the bedroom.

2. Where's the TV?
   It's in the living room.

D. Look and write.

1. Is there a TV in the bedroom?

   Yes, there is.

2. Is there a sofa in the living room?

3. Is there a bed in the kitchen?

4. Is there a TV in the bathroom?

✓

Let's Learn More _____

A. Write.

1.

2.

3.

_____
_____
_____

| in front of | next to | behind |

B. Read and check.

1. There's a stove next to the refrigerator.

☐ 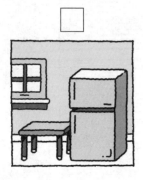 ☐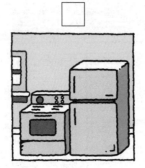

2. There's a table in front of the sofa.

☐  ☐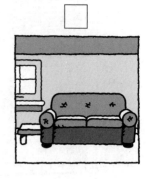

3. There are lamps behind the bed.

☐  ☐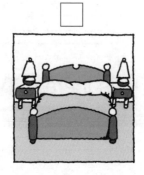

4. There are telephones in front of the window.

☐  ☐

C. Look, read, and write.

1.

Is there a bathtub next to the toilet?

No, there isn't.

2.

Is there a lamp behind the TV?

3.

Is there a telephone next to the sink?

4.

Is there a TV in front of the bed?

D. Look, read, and check.

1. Are there lamps next to the bed?
   ☐ Yes, there are. ☐ No, there aren't.

2. Are there windows behind the bed?
   ☐ Yes, there are. ☐ No, there aren't.

3. Are there telephones next to the bed?
   ☐ Yes, there are. ☐ No, there aren't.

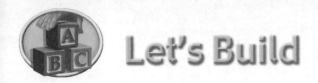

Let's Build

A. Unscramble and write.

1. the are Where books

_____ ?

_____

under table are They the

_____

_____ .

2. the Where cats are

_____ ?

_____

sofa They on the are

_____

_____ .

B. Match.

There's a cat in front of the dog.

There's a dog behind the cat!

1. There's a stove next to the refrigerator. •

2. There's a toilet behind the door. •

3. There's a bed in front of the window. •

4. There's a cat on the bed. •

• There's a window behind the bed.

• There's a bed under the cat.

There's a door in front of the toilet.

There's a refrigerator next to the stove.

C. Read and write.

1. Where's the telephone?

It's <u>on</u> the table <u>behind</u> the sofa.

2. Where's the dog?

It's ____ the box _____ the refrigerator.

3. Where's the duck?

It's ____ the sink _____ the stove.

4. Where's the bag?

It's ____ the bed _____ the window.

D. Read and check.

1. Is there a spider on the refrigerator?

☐ Yes, there is.   ☐ No, there isn't.

2. Is there a cat on the bed?

☐ Yes, there is.   ☐ No, there isn't.

3. Is there a duck in front of the sofa?

☐ Yes, there is.   ☐ No, there isn't.

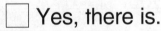
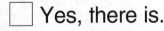

Unit 4 Things To Eat

Let's Start

A. Read and trace.

What's for lunch, Mom?

Do you want spaghetti?

Mmm. That's good. I like spaghetti.

Yes, please!

I do, too.

Spaghetti.

No, thank you!

B. Look, read, and check.

1. Do you want spaghetti?

   ☐ Yes, please.
   ☐ No, thank you.

2. Do you want a candy bar?

   ☐ Yes, please.
   ☐ No, thank you.

3. Do you want an orange?

   ☐ Yes, please.
   ☐ No, thank you.

4. Do you want ice cream?

   ☐ Yes, please.
   ☐ No, thank you.

C. Read and match.

1. Can he wink?
   Yes, he can.

2. Can she do a cartwheel?
   No, she can't.

3. Can she type?
   Yes, she can.

4. Can he play Ping-Pong?
   No, he can't.

D. Look, trace, and write.

1.

   Can he do a cartwheel?

   Yes, he can.

2.

   Can he ?

   No, he can't.

3.

   ?

   .

4.

   ?

   .

✓

Let's Learn

A. Look and write.

1.
hot chocolate

2.

3.

4.

5.

6.

7.

8.

| an omelet | a peach | a pear | a pancake |
| yogurt | cereal | tea | hot chocolate |

B. Unscramble and write.

1. a He pear wants

He wants a pear.

2. omelet wants She an

_____

3. She tea wants

_____

4. wants yogurt He

_____

C. Read, connect, and write.

1. What does she want?

2. What does she want?

3. What does he want?

She wants tea.

4. What does she want?

5. What does he want?

6. What does he want?

D. Look and check.

1. Does she want cereal?

☐ Yes, she does.

☐ No, she doesn't.

2. Does he want hot chocolate?

☐ Yes, he does.

☐ No, he doesn't.

✓

A. Find and circle.

a	p	l	f	u	r	g	p	x	o
h	a	m	b	u	r	g	e	r	s
x	n	h	w	j	m	a	a	s	t
x	c	s	t	e	w	e	c	h	o
s	a	o	p	l	w	d	h	e	r
t	k	p	a	s	d	f	e	a	k
e	e	a	g	h	b	t	s	o	u
a	s	s	x	g	r	a	p	e	s
k	s	p	a	g	h	e	t	t	i
y	v	a	s	c	h	e	e	s	e

1.

2.

3.

4.

5.

6.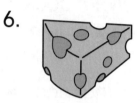

7.

8.

B. Look and write.

1.

He likes _____ .

2.

_____

_____ .

C. Read and match.

1. What does he like?
   He likes hamburgers.

2. What does she like?
   She likes grapes.

3. What does she like?
   She likes stew.

4. What does he like?
   He likes peaches.

D. Look, read, and write.

1. Does she like pancakes?
   Yes, she does.

2. Does he like _____?
   No, he doesn't.

3. _____?

4. _____?

Let's Build

A. Look and circle.

1.

She ⟨likes⟩ / doesn't like cheese.

2.

He wants / doesn't want pancakes.

3.

She wants / doesn't want an omelet.

4.

He likes / doesn't like yogurt.

B. Trace and write.

1.

He doesn't want a dog.

He wants a cat.

2.

She doesn't   rabbit.

She   frog.

3.

bird.

turtle.

C. Look, read, and write.

1.  Does she want a pear or a peach?

   She wants a peach.

2.  Does she want a giraffe or a tiger?

   _____.

3.  Does he want a camera or a music player?

   _____.

4.  Does he want a banana or a cookie?

   _____.

D. Count and write.

1.  How many eggs does she want?

   She wants three eggs.

2.  How many pancakes does he want?

   _____.

3.  How many sandwiches does she want?

   _____.

4. How many milkshakes does he want?

   _____.

✓

Units 3-4 Listen and Review

A. Read and write.

1. Where's the bed?

_____

_____

_____

2. What does he like?

_____

_____

_____

3. Where's the telephone?

_____

_____

_____

4. Does he want grapes or yogurt?

_____

_____

_____

> He likes cereal.   It's in the bedroom.
> He wants grapes.   It's next to the lamp.

B. Look and write the question.

1.

Where's the _____ ?

It's in the kitchen.

2.

_____ ?

She wants an omelet.

3.

_____ ?

He likes hamburgers.

4.

_____ ?

She wants two pears.

Let's Learn About the Months

A. Trace and number.

☐ March	☐ July
☐ September	☐ November
☐ June	☐ February
☐ December	☐ May
☐ August	☐ October
1 January	☐ April

B. Look and write.

1. What month is it?

It's February.

2. What month is it?

It's _____ .

3. What month is it?

_____ .

4. What month is it?

_____ .

 **Let's Start**

A. Write.

_____ the matter, Scott?

Maybe Mrs. Green can help you.

I'm _____.

That's too bad.

Who's _____?

Thanks for your help.

She's the new _____.

You're _____.

Get better soon!

| What's welcome sick she nurse |

B. Read and connect.

1. What's the matter? •   • That's too bad.

2. Who's she? •   • You're welcome.

3. I'm sick. •   • I'm sick.

4. Thanks for your help. •   • She's the new nurse.

C. Look and number.

1.

2.

3.

4.

☐ I make breakfast every morning.

☐ I wake up every morning.

☐ I get dressed every morning.

☐ I get out of bed every morning.

D. Trace and check.

1.

☐

☐

I get out of bed every morning.

2.

☐

☐

I get dressed every morning.

✓

Let's Learn

A. Look and write.

Who's she?

1.

   She's a nurse.

2.

3.

4.

Who's he?

5.

   He's

6.

7.

8.

a shopkeeper   a cook   a nurse   a farmer   a taxi driver
a train conductor   an office worker   a police officer

B. Connect and write.

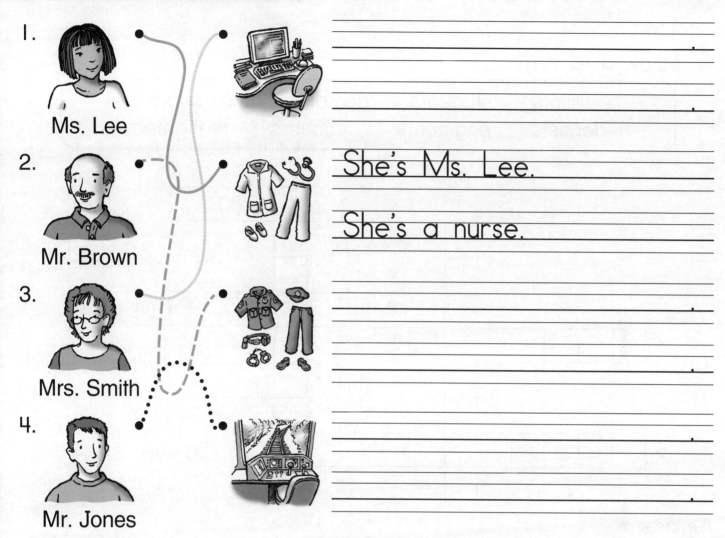

1. Ms. Lee

2. Mr. Brown

3. Mrs. Smith

4. Mr. Jones

_____
_____.
_____
_____.

She's Ms. Lee.

She's a nurse.

_____.

_____.

_____.

_____.

C. Read and match.

1. Is she a taxi driver?
   Yes, she is.

2. Is she a cook?
   No, she isn't. She's a nurse.

3. Is he a shopkeeper?
   Yes, he is.

✓

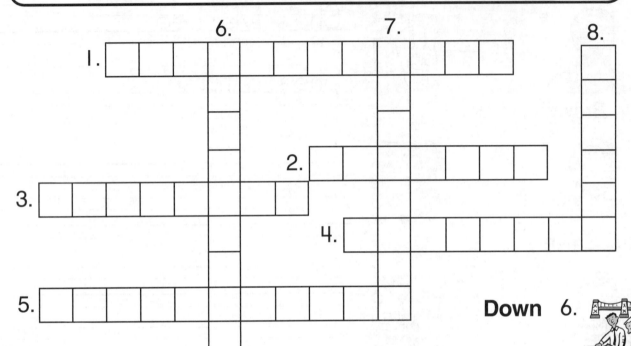

Let's Learn More _____

A. Look and write.

| pilots | students | doctors | taxi drivers |
| dentists | engineers | teachers | firefighters |

Down

Across

1.   2.   3.   4.   5.

B. Trace and write.

1.

They're teachers.

2.

C. Look and write.

Who are they?

1.

Mr. and Mrs. Smith

They're Mr. and Mrs. Smith.

They're _____.

2.

Jack and Billy Thompson

_____.

_____.

3.

Ms. Long and Ms. Park

_____.

_____.

D. Read and circle.

1. Are they teachers?

Yes, they are.
(No, they aren't.)

2. Are they doctors?

Yes, they are.
No, they aren't.

3. Are they engineers?

Yes, they are.
No, they aren't.

4. Are they dentists?

Yes, they are.
No, they aren't.

Let's Build

A. Match.

1. (I'm an engineer.) •

2. (I'm a farmer.) •

3. (I'm a firefighter.) •

B. Look and write.

1.

Mr. Ray

Who is Mr. Ray?

He's a doctor.

2.

Ms. Church

Who is _____?

She's _____.

3.

Mr. Bond

_____?

_____.

4.

Mrs. Mann

_____?

_____.

C. Read and check.

1. Is Mrs. Hill an office worker or an engineer?

☐ She's an office worker.
☐ She's an engineer.

2. Is Mr. Lee a police officer or a train conductor?

☐ He's a police officer.
☐ He's a train conductor.

3. Is Mr. Peters a pilot or a firefighter?

☐ He's a pilot.
☐ He's a firefighter.

D. Look and write.

1.

Can Mrs. Smith type?

No, she can't.

2.

Can Ben sing?

_____

3.

Can John and Bill play Ping-Pong?

_____

4.

Can Mr. Beck use chopsticks?

_____

✓

Let's Start

A. Trace and write.

1.

_____, Kate.
This is Jenny.

2.

Where are you?

_____ at home.

3.

_____ are you?

I'm at the park.

4.

Can you come to
_____?

Sure!

Where	I'm	Hi	the park

B. Connect and write.

What do you do every afternoon?

1.

2.

3. I talk on the telephone.

4.

study English   talk on the telephone   watch TV   practice the piano

C. Unscramble and write.

1. do do you afternoon What every

_____?

2. the practice I piano

_____.

3. afternoon do What every you do

_____?

4. English study I

_____.

✓

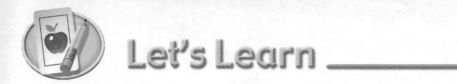

Let's Learn

A. Look and write.

1. _at school_

2. _____

3. _____

4. _____

5. _____

6. _____

at school   at work   at home   at the library   at the park   at the zoo

B. Trace and write.

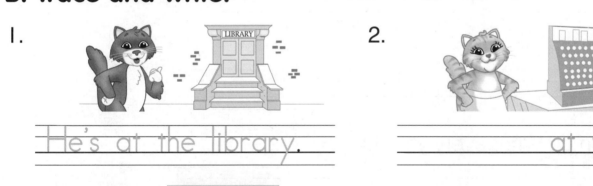

1. He's at the library.

2. _____ at work.

3. _____ school.

4. _____.

C. Find and write.

1. She's at school.

2. He's at the park.

3. _____

4. _____

5. _____

6. _____

D. Look at C. Read and check.

1. Is she at home?
   - [ ] Yes, she is.
   - [✓] No, she isn't. She's at school.

2. Is he at the library?
   - [ ] Yes, he is.
   - [ ] No, he isn't. He's at the zoo.

3. Is she at the zoo?
   - [ ] Yes, she is.
   - [ ] No, she isn't. She's at the store.

4. Is he at work?
   - [ ] Yes, he is.
   - [ ] No, he isn't. He's at home.

[✓]

Let's Learn More _____

A. Look and write.

| at the movies | at the store | in the restaurant |
| in the taxi | on the bus | on the train |

1. They're on the train.

2. They're at the

3.

4.

5.

6.

B. Read and write.

1. Where are they?

They're at the store.

2. Where are they?

_____.

3. Where are they?

_____.

4. Where are they?

_____.

C. Read, look, and circle.

1. Are they at the movies?

Yes, they are.

No, they aren't.

2. Are they on the bus?

Yes, they are.

No, they aren't.

3. Are they in the restaurant?

Yes, they are.

No, they aren't.

4. Are they in the taxi?

Yes, they are.

No, they aren't.

✓

Let's Build

A. Read and match.

1. The shopkeeper is at the store.

2. The students are at the movies.

3. The cook is in the restaurant.

4. The teachers are at the library.

B. Read and number.

1. Where's the taxi driver?
   He's in the taxi.

2. Where are the cooks?
   They're in the kitchen.

3. Where are the firefighters?
   They're in the park.

4. Where's the police officer?
   He's at the movies.

C. Look, trace, and write.

1. Is the teacher at the library?

No, he isn't.

He's at home.

2. Are the doctors in the taxi?

No, they aren't.

They're on the bus.

3. Are the farmers at home?

_____
_____
_____
_____ .

4. Is the student in the living room?

_____
_____
_____
_____ .

D. Read and match.

1. Where is the dentist?
   She's at work.

2. Where are the pilots?
   They're at the zoo.

3. Where are the farmers?
   They're at the store.

4. Where is the firefighter?
   He's on the bus.

✓

Units 5-6 Listen and Review

A. Read and match.

1. Who's she?

•   • They're Mr. and Mrs. Cross. They're farmers.

2. Where is he?

•   • Yes, he is.

3. Who are they?

•   • He's at the library.

4. Are they doctors?

•   • She's Mrs. Jones. She's the new nurse.

5. Is he at the park?

•   • No, they aren't. They're police officers.

B. Write.

1. I _____ every morning.

2. I _____ every afternoon.

3. She's at the _____.

4. He's at _____.

library
home
get dressed
watch TV

Let's Learn About the Seasons

A. Trace and write.

1.

   spring

2.

   summer

3.

   fall

4.

   winter

B. Write.

fly a kite

go skiing

go hiking

go sailing

1. What can you do in the summer?   I can go sailing.

2. What can you do in the winter?

3. What can you do in the spring?

4. What can you do in the fall?

✓

Unit 7 Doing Things

 **Let's Start**

A. Write.

Let's _____ .

What are you _____ ?

1.

2.

What are you doing?

I'm _____ .

3.

We're _____ .

| swimming |
| play a game |
| riding a bicycle |
| doing |

B. Look and write.

1. What are you doing?

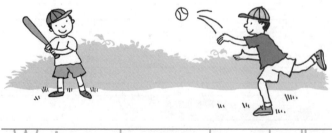

We're playing baseball.

2. What are you doing?

I'm _____ .

C. Trace and match.

1. cook dinner •

2. wash the dishes •

3. read e-mail •

4. do homework •

D. Read, trace, and write.

1.  Do you do homework every evening?

No, I don't.

2.  Do you wash the dishes every evening?

_____ .

3.  read e-mail ?

No, I don't.

4. cook dinner ?

Yes, I do.

✓

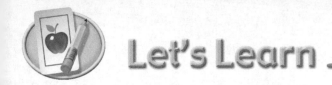

Let's Learn

A. Read and number.

1. He's coloring a picture.

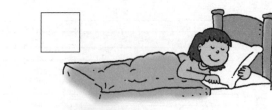

2. She's running.

3. He's dancing.

4. He's throwing a ball.

5. He's walking.

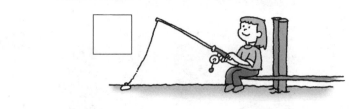

6. She's sleeping.

7. She's fishing.

8. She's singing a song.

B. Read and write.

What's he doing?

1.

He's _____ .

What's she doing?

2.

She's _____ .

3.

_____ .

4.

_____ .

C. Connect and write.

1. Is he fishing?

2. Is he throwing a ball?

3. Is she coloring a picture?

4. Is she singing a song?

_____ .

Yes, he is.

_____ .

No, he isn't.

✓

Let's Learn More

A. Read and match.

1. talking on the telephone 　　　　3. studying English

　　　　　　　2. playing soccer 　　　　　　4. watching TV

B. Trace and match.

1. They're eating apples. 　　　　　

2. They're reading comic books. 　　

3. They're riding bicycles. 　　　　

4. They're flying kites. 　　　　　

C. Write.

1.

What are they doing?

They're riding bicycles.

2.

_____?
_____.

3.

_____?
_____.

4.

_____?
_____.

D. Read and check.

1. Are they watching TV?
   ☐ Yes, they are.
   ☐ No, they aren't. They're studying English.

2. Are they reading comic books?
   ☐ Yes, they are.
   ☐ No, they aren't. They're flying kites.

3. Are they playing soccer?
   ☐ Yes, they are.
   ☐ No, they aren't. They're watching TV.

✓

Let's Build

A. Look and write.

1.

They're riding bicycles.

2.

He's _____.

3.

_____.

4.

_____.

B. Read and write the question.

1. _____ ?

He's playing soccer.

2. _____ ?

She's running.

3. _____ ?

They're flying kites.

4. _____ ?

They're eating apples.

C. Read and circle.

1. Is she walking?

Yes, she is.
~~No, she isn't.~~

2. Is he throwing a ball?

Yes, he is.
No, he isn't.

3. Are they watching TV?

Yes, they are.
No, they aren't.

4. Is he sleeping?

Yes, he is.
No, he isn't.

D. Match.

1. What is she eating?
   She's eating an omelet.

2. What are they playing?
   They're playing baseball.

3. What is she reading?
   She's reading a comic book.

4. What is he doing?
   He's doing homework.

✓

After School

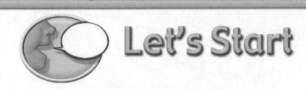

Let's Start

A. Read and number.

| | Great! See you on Sunday! |

| | Sorry. No, I can't. I'm busy. |

| | OK. See you then! |

| | Can you come over on Saturday? |

| | Sunday is OK. I'm free. |

| | What about Sunday? |

B. Read and match.

My Diary ················· **April**

SUNDAY	MONDAY	TUESDAY	WEDNESDAY	THURSDAY	FRIDAY	SATURDAY
8	9	10 go to movies	11	12 study English	13 play Ping-Pong	14 play soccer

1. Can you come over on Monday? •
2. Can you come over on Thursday? •
3. Can you come over on Sunday? •
4. Can you come over on Saturday? •

• Yes, I can. I'm free on Sunday.

• No, I can't. I'm busy on Thursday.

• Yes, I can. I'm free on Monday.

• No, I can't. I'm busy on Saturday.

C. Write.

1.

   take a bath

2.

3.

4.

take a walk   look at stars   play outside   take a bath

D. Read and check.

1.

Do you ever take a walk at night?
Yes, I do.

2.

Do you ever play outside at night?
No, I don't.

3.

Do you ever look at stars at night?
Yes, I do.

4.

Do you ever take a bath at night?
No, I don't.

✓

Let's Learn

A. Match.

1. art class •

2. English class •

3. math class •

4. soccer practice •

5. karate class •

6. piano class •

7. swimming class •

8. dance class •

B. Trace and write.

1. I go to _____ .

2. I go to _____ .

C. Look and write.

DAILY PLANNER						SEPTEMBER
SUNDAY	MONDAY	TUESDAY	WEDNESDAY	THURSDAY	FRIDAY	SATURDAY
4	5	6	7	8	9	10
art class	Karate class	English class	swimming class	Soccer practice	math class	dance class

1. What do you do on Fridays?

   I go to math class.

2. What do you do on Mondays?

   I go to _____.

3. What do you do on Tuesdays?

   _____.

4. _____?

   I go to swimming class.

5. _____?

   I go to dance class.

6. _____?

   I go to art class.

D. How about you? Write.

1. **What do you do on Saturdays?**

   _____.

2. **What do you do on Tuesdays?**

   _____.

Let's Learn More

A. Look and write.

1.

walk the dog

2.

3.

4.

take a bath　walk the dog　do homework　go to the bookstore

B. Read and match.

1. He practices the piano
after school.

2. She rides a bicycle
after school.

3. He listens to music
after school.

4. She talks on the telephone
after school.

C. Look and write.

1.

What does she do after school?

She _____ .

2.

What does he do after school?

_____ .

3.

_____ ?

_____ .

4.

_____ ?

_____ .

D. Look and check.

1.

Does he study English after school?

☐ Yes, he does.

☐ No, he doesn't.

2.

Does she do homework after school?

☐ Yes, she does.

☐ No, she doesn't.

Let's Build

A. Read and draw a line.

1. 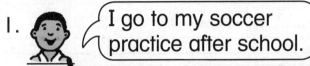 I go to my soccer practice after school.

2. I go to my dance class after school.

3. I go to my art class after school.

4. I go to my piano class after school.

B. Look and write.

1.

He goes to his math class after school.

2.

She goes to her _____.

3.

_____

_____.

C. Look and write.

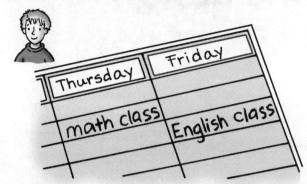

1. What does he do on Fridays?

   He goes to English class.

2. What does he do on Thursdays?

   _____

   _____.

3. What does she do on Wednesdays?

   _____

   _____.

4. What does she do on Tuesdays?

   _____

   _____.

D. What about you? Write.

What do you do after school on Fridays?

I go to the bookstore. What about you?

1. What do you do after school on Tuesdays?

   _____

   _____.

2. What do you do after school on Wednesdays?

   _____

   _____.

3. Do you ever go to soccer practice after school?

   _____

   _____.

✓

Units 7-8 Listen and Review

A. Write.

1. Are they doing homework?

   _____
   _____
   _____

2. Is she coloring a picture?

   _____
   _____
   _____

3. What does he do after school on Fridays?

   _____
   _____
   _____

4. What are they doing?

   _____
   _____
   _____

B. Match.

1. look at stars •

2. eat apples •

3. walk the dog •

4. play outside •

5. wash the dishes •

6. take a bath •

Let's Learn About Time

A. Read and write.

1. It's two-fifteen.

   It's 2:15.

2. It's twelve-thirty.

   It's _____.

3. It's four o'clock.

   _____.

4. It's nine forty-five.

   _____.

5. It's twelve midnight.

   _____.

6. It's twelve noon.

   _____.

B. Read, write, and check.

1. It's eight o'clock in the morning.

2. It's two thirty in the afternoon.

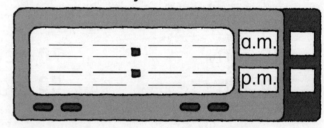

3. It's five o'clock in the afternoon.

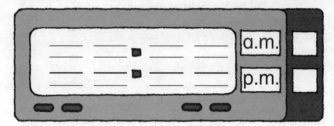

4. It's seven forty-five at night.

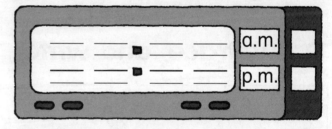

5. It's three thirty in the morning.

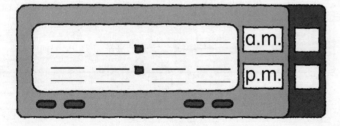

6. It's eleven o'clock at night.

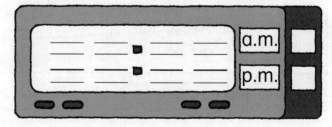

Number Practice

1 one	11 eleven	21 twenty-one
2 two	12 twelve	22 twenty-two
3 three	13 thirteen	23 twenty-three
4 four	14 fourteen	24 twenty-four
5 five	15 fifteen	25 twenty-five
6 six	16 sixteen	26 twenty-six
7 seven	17 seventeen	27 twenty-seven
8 eight	18 eighteen	28 twenty-eight
9 nine	19 nineteen	29 twenty-nine
10 ten	20 twenty	30 thirty

40 forty	70 seventy	90 ninety
50 fifty	80 eighty	100 one hundred
60 sixty		

Draw, trace, and write.

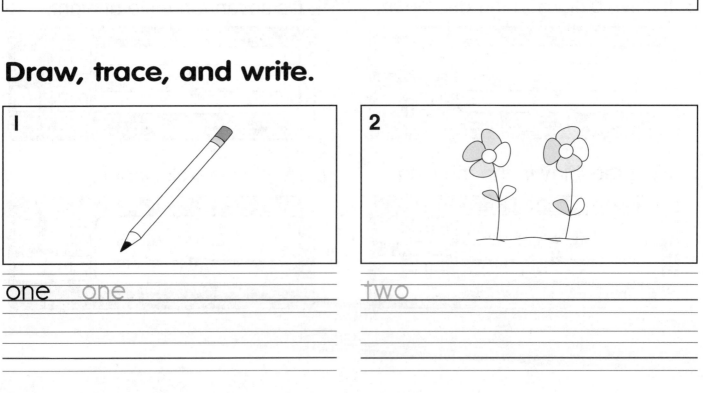

1

2

one   one

two

3

three

4

four

5

five

6

six

7

seven

8

eight

✓

9

nine

10

ten

11

eleven

12

twelve

13

thirteen

14

fourteen

15

fifteen

16

sixteen

17

seventeen

18

eighteen

19

nineteen

20

twenty

✓

Count, trace, and write.

21	22
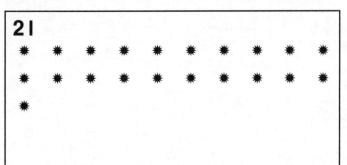	

twenty—one

twenty—two

23	24
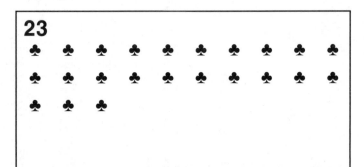	

twenty—three

twenty—four

25	26
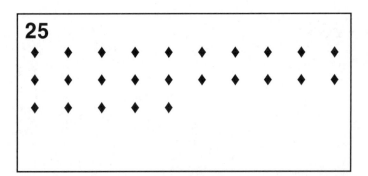	

twenty—five

twenty—six

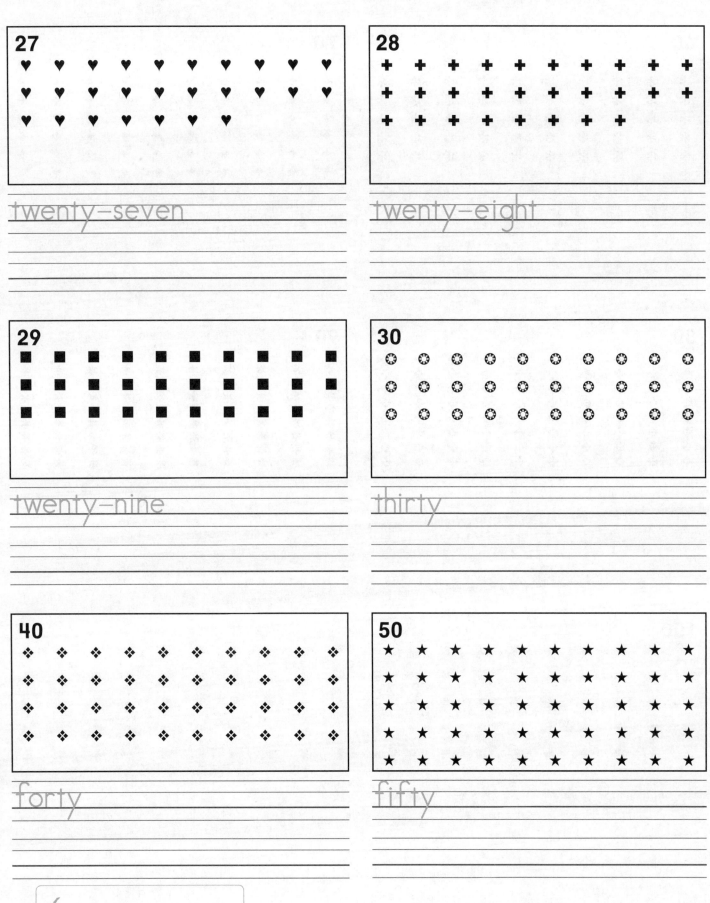

27

twenty–seven

28

twenty–eight

29

twenty–nine

30

thirty

40

forty

50

fifty

60

sixty

70

seventy

80

eighty

90

ninety

100

one hundred